Plants

Ferns

June Loves

An Imprint of Chelsea House Publishers
A Haights Cross Communications Company

Philadelphia

This edition first published in 2005 in the United States of America by Chelsea House Publishers, a subsidiary of Haights Cross Communications.

All rights reserved. No part of this publication may be reproduced or transmitted in any form or by any means without the written permission of the publisher.

Chelsea House Publishers
2080 Cabot Boulevard West, Suite 201
Langhorne, PA 19047-1813

The Chelsea House world wide web address is www.chelseahouse.com

First published in 2005 by
MACMILLAN EDUCATION AUSTRALIA PTY LTD
627 Chapel Street, South Yarra, Australia 3141

Visit our website at www.macmillan.com.au

Associated companies and representatives throughout the world.

Copyright © June Loves 2005

Library of Congress Cataloging-in-Publication Data
Loves, June.
  Ferns / June Loves.
  p. cm. – (Plants)
  Includes index.
  ISBN 0-7910-8267-9
  1. Ferns – Juvenile literature. I. Title.
  QK522.5.L68 2004
  587'.3–dc22

2004016334

Edited by Anna Fern
Text and cover design by Christine Deering
Page layout by Christine Deering
Photo research by Legend Images
Illustrations by Melissa Webb

Printed in China

Acknowledgements

The author and the publisher are grateful to the following for permission to reproduce copyright material:

Cover photograph: Ferns in a forest, courtesy of Photodisc.

Ferrero-Labat/AUSCAPE, p. 13; C. Andrew Henley/AUSCAPE, pp. 3, 20; Tom & Therisa Stack/AUSCAPE, p. 30; Australian National Botanic Gardens, p. 15; Australian Picture Library, pp. 22, 27; The DW Stock Picture Library, p. 8; Fred Hirschmann, p. 28; Brett Dennis/Lochman Transparencies, p. 7; Jiri Lochman/Lochman Transparencies, pp. 9, 10, 11, 21; Heather Angel/Natural Visions, p. 29; Photodisc, pp. 1, 4, 6, 23; Steve Lovegrove/Picture Tasmania Photo Library, pp. 5, 12, 14, 26.

While every care has been taken to trace and acknowledge copyright, the publisher tenders their apologies for any accidental infringement where copyright has proved untraceable. Where the attempt has been unsuccessful, the publisher welcomes information that would redress the situation.

Contents

Plants	4
Where Ferns Grow	6
Kinds of Ferns	8
Parts of Ferns	14
How Ferns Grow	16
Growing Ferns	22
Grow a Fern and Moss Garden	24
Tips for Gardeners	26
Useful Ferns	28
Amazing Ferns	30
Glossary	31
Index	32

Plants

Plants are living things. They grow all over the world, in hot and cold places.

Many different plants live in forests.

Ferns

Ferns are plants with beautiful **fronds**, or leaves. Most ferns have collections of small velvety **spore cases** underneath their fronds.

Ferns do not have flowers.

Where Ferns Grow

Ferns grow in most places, except the coldest and driest areas. They do not need as much light or soil as some other plants to grow. Ferns grow in damp, shady areas in soil, on rocks, or on other plants.

Ferns grow in cool forests and woodlands.

Ferns grow very well in **rain forests**, where there is plenty of rain and shade.

Some ferns grow very well in hot, damp rain forests.

Kinds of Ferns

There are many different kinds of ferns. They have many different shapes and sizes. Some ferns are small, and grow to just a few inches. Other ferns can grow as tall as trees.

These ferns have very large fronds.

Fern Fronds

Some ferns have fronds that are a simple shape. Other fern fronds are divided into small leaflets.

Maidenhair ferns have delicate fronds.

Tree Ferns

Tree ferns have strong, woody stems. Large fronds grow at the top of the woody stems.

Tree ferns can grow into trees that are many feet high.

Water Ferns

Water ferns float on the surface of lakes and ponds. Their **roots** dangle in the water.

Water ferns look very different from most ferns.

Bracken

Bracken is a fern that grows all over the world. In some places it is a **weed**. Bracken has underground roots which spread quickly.

Bracken can be a pest when it spreads onto farmland.

Elephant Ferns

The fronds of the elephant fern can be very large. They often reach up to 26 feet (8 meters) in length.

Elephant ferns have large, feathery fronds and grow on other trees in rain forests.

Parts of Ferns

The roots and stems of ferns usually grow underground, and the fronds grow above the ground.

umbrella-like fronds

marks where the fronds fall off as the fern grows

strong woody stem

roots hold the fern in the soil and absorb **nutrients**

Tree ferns grow in damp, shady forests.

Most ferns have small spore cases underneath their fronds. The spore cases contain **spores**, which will grow into new ferns.

spore case contains spores

This is a closer view of the frond of a tree fern.

How Ferns Grow

Ferns grow from tiny seed-like spores.

Millions of spores grow in tiny spore cases underneath a fern's fronds. When the spore cases break, the spores scatter on the wind like fine dust.

When a spore falls to the ground, it grows into a tiny, heart-shaped plant called a **prothallium.**

new fern

prothallium will shrivel up

A new fern plant grows from the prothallium.

How a Prothallium Grows into a Fern

Each prothallium that grows from a spore produces male **cells** and female cells. For the prothallium to continue growing into a fern, a male cell and a female cell need to join together.

female cells are made here

prothallium

male cells are made here

root-like threads hold the prothallium in the soil

A spore grows into a prothallium.

When water is present, the male cells swim to the female cells and they join together. This is called **fertilization**. After fertilization, a new fern begins to grow.

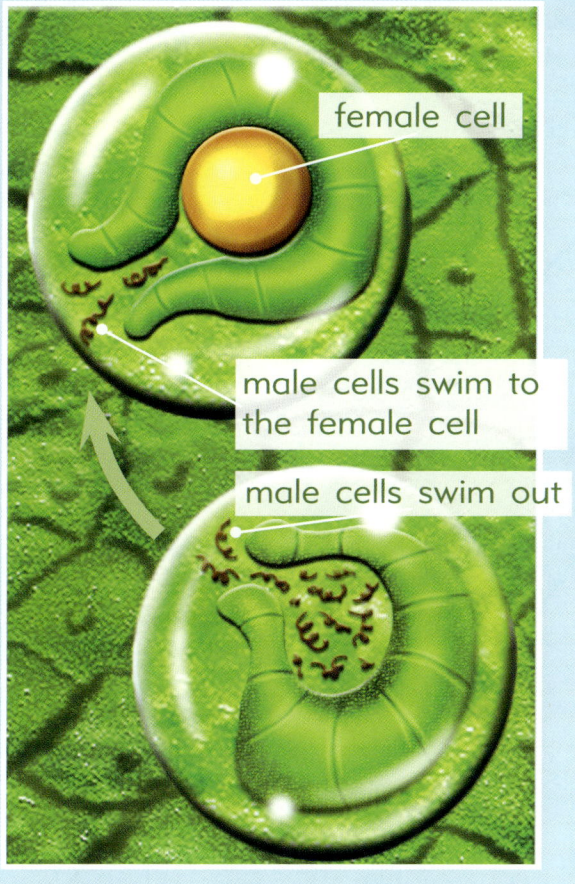

female cell

male cells swim to the female cell

male cells swim out

new fern grows

prothallium disappears

A new fern begins to grow.

How Fern Fronds Grow

New fern fronds are curled up tightly. As they grow, they slowly uncurl.

Curled-up fern fronds are sometimes called fiddleheads, because they look like the curled end of a violin, or fiddle.

Helpers for Ferns

Some ferns grow on trees and on other strong plants for support. The ferns do not harm the supporting plant.

These ferns have attached themselves to a tree, but they will not harm the tree.

Growing Ferns

Many ferns are grown in plant nurseries and are sold as potted plants. You can grow ferns in pots, or plant them in the garden. Like other plants, ferns need soil, water, and light to grow.

The ferns in this nursery are kept warm and moist so that they will thrive.

Many ferns grow best in damp, shady places and do not like hot sunshine. A layer of **mulch** helps keep the soil around ferns damp.

Mosses and fallen leaves make a layer of mulch around this fern.

Grow a Fern and Moss Garden

Use a glass container to grow a fern and moss garden.

What you need:
- a fish tank or large jar
- small, clean stones
- damp soil
- pieces of rock for decoration
- ferns and mosses
- a spray watering container

What to do:

1 Line the bottom of the container with small stones.

2 Add a thick layer of moist soil and plant your ferns and mosses.

3 Arrange pieces of rock among the plants.

4 Water your garden and place it away from direct sunlight.

Tips for Gardeners

Ferns are fun to grow in pots or in the garden.

- Some ferns grow well outdoors in sunlight, while others grow best in shade. Make sure your ferns are growing in the right place.
- Keep your ferns moist by watering them regularly.

Ferns need to be watered regularly to stay healthy.

- Check the roots of your potted ferns when they have grown. If the roots look tangled, move your plant to a bigger pot, or plant it in the garden.
- Always wash your hands and scrub your nails when you have finished handling soil.

These ferns grow well in a sheltered place, out of the hot sun.

Useful Ferns

The young fronds of some ferns can be cooked and eaten as a green vegetable. The inside core of tree ferns is also edible.

This woman is collecting fiddlehead ferns to eat.

For thousands of years, people all over the world have used ferns to make medicine. Today scientists are researching ways to use ferns for medicine. Ferns can even be used as a building material.

Tree ferns have been used to make this traditional building in New Zealand.

Amazing Ferns

Ferns were one of the first plants to grow on Earth. They first grew about 300 million years ago and the remains can be seen today in the form of **fossils**.

The frond of a fern that lived millions of years ago has been preserved as a fossil in this rock.

Glossary

cell — tiny building block of a living thing

fertilization — joining together of male cells and female cells to form a new plant

fossil — the remains of a plant or animal that have been in the ground for a very long time

frond — a feathery leaf

mulch — a layer of chopped-up leaves or other plant material to help stop the soil from drying out and stop weeds from growing

nutrients — food in the soil that a plant can use to grow

prothallium — small delicate plant which grows from a spore which can produce another plant, such as a fern

rain forest — a thick forest with heavy rainfall, and which is full of living things

root — part of a plant that grows down into the soil and takes in water and nutrients

spore — a tiny cell made by ferns that can grow into a new plant

spore case — small container under the leaf of a fern which holds spores

weed — a plant that is growing where it is not wanted

Index

- **b** building materials, 29
- **c** climate, 4, 6–7
- **f** fertilization, 18–19
  flowers, 5
  food, 28
  fossils, 30
- **g** gardening, 22–27
- **l** leaves, 5, 8–9, 13, 14–15, 20, 28
  life cycle, 16–19
- **m** medicine, 29
  mulch, 23
- **p** plants, 4
  pot plants, 22, 27
  prothallia, 17–19
- **r** rain forests, 7, 13
  roots, 11, 12, 14, 21
- **s** soil, 6, 22, 23, 27
  spores, 5, 15, 16–18
  stems, 10, 14
  sunlight, 6, 23, 26
- **w** water, 6, 7, 11, 19, 22, 23, 26
  weeds, 12

Back cover
Stain noted.
YRK 8/3/23